The Book On
Going Green

Have a Better Life
Through Smarter Living

The Book On
Going Green

Have a Better Life
Through Smarter Living

EVAN ALBRIGHT

KingsHill Publishing,
23852 Pacific Coast Highway #384, Malibu, CA 90265

Visit our Web site at http://www.evanalbright.com
Register for regular updates at: www.TheGreenLivingeExpo.com

ISBN: 978-0-6152-2273-8

Printed in the United States of America
First Printing: June 2008

To Becky
Jami, Ryan, Chris, Sagan,
Jess & Patty

And the loving support
from Eco-Sapians throughout
The world

Special thanks to
Shannon Dauphin

Contents

Introduction

Going green seems to be an appropriate topic, after all; you can't open a newspaper, listen to the radio or watch television without seeing a story about ways to better our environment. It seems everyone and their brother has joined the cause. Every business, school, organization, and government agency is rushing as fast as they can to prove how green they are. It's become a fad, a cool thing to do, and in many ways, a competition.

Do you want to build a house? You can go green! Are you going on vacation? Make sure it's a green one! Are you dead and need to be buried? You can still go green! That's right — as amazing as it sounds, even funeral homes are now advertising the green alternative.

It's everywhere now, in every corner of our lives. But where did this "going green" mind-set come from in the first place?

A recent study conducted by the National Chamber of Commerce showed that while 80% of the people surveyed recognized "go green" and related terminology, over 70% of them didn't have a clear understanding of what going green really was! Most knew it had something to do with building but didn't relate it to any specific action in their daily lives.

It's interesting that everyone seems to be talking about going green, but nobody is bothering to explain what it means.

Unfortunately, that leaves much of the education up to those who have an agenda. Many of these so-called environmental groups spend a good portion of their time figuring out how to get their message out and how to convert people to their point of view.

One of the major reasons cited by environmental activists for going green is the Global Warming issue. They say we need to slow Global Warming, or stop it altogether. The mantra of "do anything we can, just do it quick and stop this horrible catastrophe that man has brought upon himself" is usually followed by some type of program that will limit a person's choices, or worse, tax and fine them for behavior that isn't considered environmentally correct.

Though some have tried to draw parallels, the environmental movement of today isn't anything like the hippie movement of the 1960s and 70s. Free Love and Peace on Earth has been replaced with finger-wagging elitists who believe their views are so superior to everyone else that it's inappropriate to question them or, God forbid, express an opposite opinion.

Global Warming became the environmental flavor of the month after many environmentalists realized that Acid Rain, the destruction of the Tropical Rainforest and the polluted waters of the Amazon didn't have that special "in your gut punch" that they needed to sustain a worldwide cause-celeb. They needed something to really pull on the heartstrings and more importantly, dig into the wallets of those who felt the pain. Enter Global Warming! It has everything. We all live on the planet and the problem is Global! Every man, woman and child has the golden opportunity to dig into their wallets and help the cause.

Who doesn't want to help a drowning polar bear?

This is why we see governments all over the world rushing to find ways to implement changes that show just how "green" they are. Money doesn't appear to be a problem. Governments can simply raise taxes, after all, it's a great cause and thanks to the steady drumbeat of the media, nobody seems to mind. Global Warming is the perfect storm of catastrophe that will propel many obscure and unknown environmental causes to the top of the funding heap and keep the money rolling in for years to come.

What's been lost in all these hysterics about Global Warming is one simple fact.

We may find that man made Global Warming doesn't exist.

I know, Al Gore who appears to be an authority on everything from the birth of the Internet to Global Warming claims that we're doomed if we don't act today, and many scientists have agreed with his view, but the fact remains that many scientists who are equally credible, believe Global Warming is a myth.

As unpopular as it may sound, the jury is still out on Global Warming. I've been assailed by environmentalists who are shocked that a full fledged green blooded environmentalist like myself would have the audacity to profess that Global Warming may be a myth, but so be it. I operate under the assumption that the truth will set you free, and after all, it's important to remember, whether Global Warming is real or not, it still makes sense to help preserve the planet by going green.

Remember those hippies who preached loving the planet? They were right, even way back then. Today's environmental movement is being hijacked by a swarm of Johnny-come-lately's who are trying to get their fifteen minutes of fame, riding on the backs of those individuals who do truly care for and want to preserve our planet. We don't need the bogeyman of Global Warming to realize we need to leave the planet in better shape than it was when we arrived. Anyone who believes we should foul our air, pollute our water and pump acid into the ground to contaminate the very food we eat is, frankly, an idiot – Global Warming or not!

Going green just makes sense. Reducing the carbon dioxide and methane gas we put into the air makes sense. Drinking clean water and eating organic food makes sense. Designing our homes to use less energy makes sense. Switching from cleaning supplies filled with chemicals to organic cleaning supplies that are good for the environment makes sense.

This book is dedicated to making sense. It's dedicated to showing you ways you can Go Green, improve your life and live better by living smarter.

There are many people who believe Global Warming is as real as the air we breathe. They may be right or they may be wrong.

However, regardless of where the truth lies, it still makes sense to Go Green. You can have a better life through smarter living!

The Book On
Going Green

Have a Better Life
Through Smarter Living

Why Go Green?

Why Go Green?

As I've stated in the introduction to this book, going green just make sense. It's important to the environment, but not only that, it's important to us as residents of this planet. The amount of waste we produce every year, every week, or even on a daily basis is staggering by anyone's standard.

But do you know how much that is? It's easy to put facts and figures out there, but what do they really mean? Most people who read information about going green simply skim over the numbers, because they can't relate to them.

Maybe these facts and figures will help bring it all a little closer to home.

The amount of wood and paper we throw away each year is enough to heat 50 million homes for 20 years. To put those numbers in perspective, that's enough to heat all the homes in California and Florida – combined – for two decades.

Over 100 million Americans breathe air so polluted, the federal government has deemed it unsafe.

You know those Styrofoam coffee cups? The ones you find in almost every office? Americans alone toss away 25 billion of those every year – and they are not biodegradable.

But it gets worse. Americans throw away 2.5 million plastic

beverage bottles an hour. That's 60 million every single day. Now imagine how many bottles are thrown away over the course of a year...the number doesn't even register on most calculators.

We go through over 60 million beverage cans in a year. Most of those are not recycled. To put it in perspective, imagine a line of cans to the moon – then multiply that by 20 times, and that's how much we throw away.

The sad part is that at least 84% of kitchen trash is recyclable. How much of it does the average person recycle? None!

Before you buy...ask these questions:

- Is this something I really need?
- Is this something I could get somewhere else, perhaps from a neighbor or a recycling exchange?
- Is there another product, perhaps one that I already have, that would perform the same function?
- How would I dispose of this item? Is it something that could be recycled when I'm finished with it?
- What goes into making this? Am I contributing to pollution by purchasing this product?
- Where was this made – and under what circumstances?
- Are the materials in this product renewable? Were they harvested in a sustainable manner?

Unfortunately, we live in a disposable society. Something is broken? Throw it out! Don't need something anymore? Get rid of it! You would rather have a different color sweater for this year? Throw out the old one! You can always buy something new.

That's the problem. We're always buying something new, but what happens to what we had before? It goes straight into a landfill, and from there it disintegrates – either slowly, or quickly. It eventually pollutes our land, our water, and our air.

We can step out of the cycle of the disposable society. Instead of buying something new, why not find it elsewhere? Join a recycling group and get what you need, gently used. If you don't want something anymore, share it with someone else. If something is broken, can it be repaired? If it can't be repaired, can it be used for something else?

A good friend of mine had a radio that didn't work anymore. Instead of throwing it out, he cut open the top of it, cleaned out the inside, and made a lovely, unique flower pot for his wife. It was an old item with a new lease on life!

If you really believe you need something new, decide what you are going to give back in exchange for it. How can you give back to your community to offset the new item you just purchased? Maybe you could donate mulch or compost to your local farmer's co-op.

If you begin to view things differently, you can step out of that "disposable society" mold – and the environment will be all the better for it!

The Book On
Going Green

Have a Better Life
Through Smarter Living

It All Begins at Home

It All Begins at Home

It makes sense to go green, and it also makes sense to start with the things you can change today. Every little bit helps the environment, and helps you and your family live healthier, too. If that weren't enough, just wait until you start to see the results! The feeling of satisfaction and well-being will be more than enough to spur you to more and better changes.

Recently, we had an opportunity to change all of our cleaning products for our home to non-VOC (volatile organic compound) cleaners. The difference was immediate. Our home didn't have that chemical, disinfectant smell that comes with your run of the mill, off the shelf, grocery store cleaners. Spic and Span may have worked for your mother but today there are many options for natural, organic based cleaners that work just as well, but don't make your house smell like your local dog kennel. Try it, you'll see. You will have a very clean, natural smelling home that will be a joy to relax in.

Going green begins with you. What better place to start than the place you spend the majority of your time? Let's look at some tips to going green for your home.

General Tips for Your Home

Remember when your mother yelled at you to turn off the lights when you left a room? She had the right idea. It is a very simple thing to do, but it works. Turn off the lights when leave a room, and only turn them on when you really need them. The natural light streaming through your windows should be enough during the day.

Replace your regular light bulbs with compact fluorescents. You've probably seen them – they are the lights that look like delicate curly-cues. They aren't delicate at all! They last much longer than the usual bulbs, and they put out more light while using less energy. In fact, they use up to 75% less energy for the same amount of light, and can last ten times longer than your old bulbs.

The initial investment in these bulbs is made up by the savings on your electric bill. An added bonus: the fact that the compact fluorescents last so long means less light bulbs will clog up the landfills.

Choose the right type of fluorescent bulb for your fixtures. There are many varieties, so make sure you read the information on each one to determine which kind will be most efficient in the different rooms of your home.

What do you do with those old light bulbs that still work? Donate them for use in your local Goodwill store, and encourage them to replace them with compact fluorescents when they burn out. To be charitable, you could even donate CFL's to the thrift store, to support the effort.

It's a good idea to avoid anything battery operated. The batteries are not easy to recycle, and most communities don't have facilities to do it. If you use batteries, make sure they are rechargeable or better yet, solar batteries.

Also avoid the use of polyvinyl chloride in your home. This is also known as PVC or vinyl. The entire cycle of these products is harmful to the environment, and it's also harmful to you. They pollute your home just by being in there! PVC items can include shower curtains, pipes, flooring, and even children's toys. Avoid them if at all possible!

Do not use aerosols. You can tell just by spraying them that they use a ton of chemicals, and none of those are good for the air. Think about what you breathe in when you inhale the after-mist of these products. It's scary to consider what chemicals might be drawn into your body with every breath you take.

Don't use the traditional WD-40 and other solvents to ease a squeaky door or lubricate switches. Use castor oil or mineral oil instead.

Did you know that appliances draw power even when they aren't turned on? Simply being plugged into an outlet means a small amount of electricity is flowing to the appliance. It happens with everything from cell phone chargers to televisions to hair dryers. Eliminate this "phantom load" on your energy bill by unplugging everything when it isn't in use.

Making this a habit comes with a bonus: During thunderstorms or lightning storms, power surges through the electrical system won't affect any of your appliances, as long as they are unplugged!

Insulate your home. It helps keep it warm in the winter, cool in the summer, and allows you to use less fuel to make your home comfortable. Look into environmentally-conscious insulation, and if you are replacing your old insulation, find a good recycling program for the material you will be pulling out of the house. Perhaps even recycle it by donating it to a home that needs extra insulation. Extreme versions include 'Jean material' and/or hay product.

Weather stripping and caulking are cheap ways to make sure your home is insulated even further. The caulk is permanent and helps keep air leaks from forming around windows. Your doors will be sealed securely with weather stripping, allowing even more conservation of heat and energy.

Open your curtains wide during the day and let the sunlight in. This might be all the warmth you need. When evening comes, close the curtains tightly to help keep all that heat inside.

As our ancestors did, close up and cover the windows in the winter to help keep the heat inside your home. Make use of "draft dodgers" – long sacks filled with sand or gravel that rest snugly against the bottom of your doors to prevent any air from coming in under the weather stripping.

If you don't use all of your house, close off the extra rooms. If there is less space to heat or cool, there is less energy used.

If you have a pool in your yard, a one-time investment of a solar pool cover, easily heats the pool. Easy to remove, the cover also helps to keep the pool clean. Dark bottom pools—tiles in dark blue or black, attract the sun and automatically warm the pool with the rays of the sun.

Change your furnace filters once a month. More energy is consumed when your heater has to operate with dust all over it. Making it easier to breathe is going to make it easier to heat the home, which means less energy is used.

Conserve fuel by turning down the thermostat. If you're a bit chilly, put on a sweater instead of turning up the heat. While you are away from home, turn your thermostat down. You need to make sure the pipes don't freeze, but does it really need to be warm in your house for any other reason?

If things are a bit warm in the house, try putting a fan in the window instead of cranking up the air conditioner.

If you must use an air conditioner in your home, follow these tips to keep it running at maximum efficiency:

Turn it down! Run it on the lowest possible setting that keeps things comfortable. 78 degrees is our recommended setting for the summer, 68 degrees for the winter.

Turn off the air conditioning in rooms you don't use. If you use window units, close off the doors to the rooms you don't use, and if you have a central air unit, seal off the vents in those unoccupied areas.

Clean or replace the filters. Generally, once a month is what a manufacturer recommends. A clean, well-maintained system doesn't have to work as hard, and thus uses less power.

Replace the hot, incandescent lights in your home with the lower-impact, efficient compact fluorescents.

Keep your air conditioner on a timer. Program it to turn off when the house is empty and to turn on a few minutes before you are set to arrive back home. This will keep the house cool only when necessary.

Cut the heat from the sun by putting blinds on your windows, or use UV-blocking film. Install awnings, or plant trees around your home to shade the house and keep the cool inside.

From time to time, bring in a professional to look at your air conditioning unit. A licensed contractor can make sure your system is working properly, and can give you tips on how to make it work even better.

Update your flooring by replacing your 'toxic' carpet filled with chemicals to bamboo or hardwood flooring. Make sure it is eco-friendly, and not treated with harsh chemicals that will fill up your home. Bamboo is a sustainable resource as it only takes approximately one year to grow. There are hardwood manufacturers going against 'deforestation' and are committed in providing the best in recycled flooring.

If you need to replace your air conditioner, look into appliances with the Energy-Star rating. Look for units that have a higher EER (Energy Efficient Ratio) or SEER (Seasonal Energy Efficient Ratio). The higher the number, the more effective they are in conserving energy. The higher number on your appliance might mean it costs more – but it pays for itself over and over during the life of the appliance.

Make sure the unit you have is the right size! Measure the rooms in your house and make sure you aren't buying an air conditioner that is too big for the area. On the other hand, an air conditioner that is too small will work extra hard to cool the rooms, which means more power will be used.

Ceiling fans offer more than a decorative touch to your home, they use 90% less energy than typical air conditioning units. Those built with the energy star rating save 50% more than traditional ceiling fans.

Finally, don't hesitate to get several estimates on what it will cost to cool your home, and have it reevaluated from time to time. The evaluation will help you save money.

On the flip-side, if you have a furnace, fireplace, or gas heater, make sure they are regularly serviced. Keeping them in good repair not only makes them more efficient and uses less energy, it helps prevent deadly fumes. Turn gas heaters down to 120 degrees in the summer, since hot showers are needed less in the summertime. To be safety conscious, install a carbon monoxide detector – and make sure it is one of the very few things in your home that you never unplug!

Turn off your computer when not in use. Computers generate a large amount of heat, which will save in electricity costs.

Furnish your home with furniture made out of natural fibers or materials. They are made in more environmentally-friendly ways, will last longer and can almost always be recycled. Look for furniture made of wood, metals or glass, or natural fibers like hemp and wicker.

When painting your house, choose water-based latex paints. Don't use solvent-based paints! Never use lead based paints, either. Not only are they bad for the environment, they are bad for your health.

When you do paint your home, make sure it's well-ventilated. In fact, whether you are painting or not, make sure your home has good ventilation and balanced humidity. This prevents the growth of mold and mildew, which is not only harmful to your house, but to your health as well.

In the Kitchen

Keep a container of water in your refrigerator. When you want a drink, it's already cold – and you don't have to turn on the tap!

Always use reusable items. Avoid buying foods in plastic packaging, and look instead for foods in glass jars or environmentally-friendly materials.

Avoid storing your foods in plastic, too. If you must do this, use plastic containers made specifically for that purpose, as they can be used over and over again.

But never microwave food in plastic containers! Why? Even the plastics that are safe for food storage and are listed as "microwavable" contain chemicals that can leach into your food when it is heated. To be certain that your food is hot without any added chemicals to make it that way, heat food in glass containers or on plates.

Can you think of creative ways to reuse your glass jars? Perhaps they can serve as lunch containers. Depending on the kind of glass and the seal of the lid, you might be able to recycle the jars for canning vegetables.

Use cloths for cleaning instead of paper napkins and paper towels.

Compost your food waste and use it as natural fertilizer for your lawn. A simple pot with a lid can be used as a kitchen composter. Fill it up with your kitchen scraps, and take it outside once a week to dump on the compost pile.

If you have leftover food, such as meats or fruits, that aren't appropriate for the compost pile, feed them to the animals! Birds love any kind of leftover fruit. Leftover meats might make a nice treat for your household pets.

Your appliances take up a huge amount of energy. In fact, some statistics say the refrigerator alone is responsible for 7% of the power consumption in the United States. If you can find a way to reduce the power your appliances use, the world will benefit just as much as your bank account will.

Start by comparing the energy ratings of appliances. All appliances are required to have this information on a sticker somewhere on the front. These stickers will tell you how many kilowatts of energy the appliances uses every month. Obviously, you will always want to go with the lowest energy rating.

Here are some tips to save energy with your refrigerator:

Don't place your refrigerator near your stove or in direct sunlight. In fact, don't place it anywhere near a heat source, even a natural one. The cooler the air around it, the easier the work to keep the inside cold.

Open the door as little as possible, and when you do open it, make it quick. This helps hold the cold air inside and conserves energy.

The condenser coils on the back of your refrigerator collect dust, and this makes your appliance inefficient. Vacuum or clean the coils every six months to keep the refrigerator running at its best.

Keep the fridge at 38-24 degrees Fahrenheit (3-5 degrees Celsius). The freezer should be kept between 0 and 5 degrees Fahrenheit (-17 to -15 Celsius). This will provide maximum cooling while making sure your appliance stays as efficient as possible.

Keep the door gasket clean. It should create a tight seal when the door is closed. Feel around the gasket from time to time; if you feel a draft of cold air, it's time to clean, repair or replace the gasket.

Tips for using your stove top and oven:

Consider electric kettles for boiling water. They use half the energy needed to boil it on the stove. If this isn't feasible, make sure to put a lid on the pot while you are boiling water. A pot with a lid boils much faster. And finally, turn down the heat after the water boils. A lightly rolling boil cooks just as well as a hard, raging boil.

Pressure cookers use very little energy. The same goes with slow cookers. Not only do these appliances save energy, they free up your time, too.

Cooking food in glass dishes is better than using metal pans. Make sure the bottom of your pan is the same size as your burner, to maximize efficiency in cooking.

Do you always preheat your oven? It's probably not necessary. When baking pastries and cakes, preheat for about ten minutes. Otherwise, don't bother. Also, turn your oven off about 15 minutes early for casseroles or roasts. The heat trapped in the oven will be enough to finish the job.

Don't peek at your food as it is cooking! Lifting the lid of a slow cooker or opening the door of the oven lets out heat, and it takes a while for the appliance to build it back up. The less you open the door, the faster your food cooks, and the more energy you save.

Thaw out your food before you cook it. Thawed food takes much less energy to cook.

Do you have a dishwasher? Don't use it at all if you can avoid it. If you do decide to use it, make sure the racks are full, and run it on the economy cycle. Don't use the heating cycle; the dishes will dry just fine on their own if you leave them overnight, especially if you set the door slightly ajar to allow the water to evaporate faster.

When you do dishes in the sink, don't keep the water running. You will go through gallon after gallon this way, and never realize the amount you are wasting. Fill up the sink with the water you need to wash dishes, and once you're done washing them, rinse them all at once, instead of one at a time.

In the Bathroom

When you're thinking of ways to save energy in the bathroom, one of your first thoughts will be about all the pipes under the floor. How can you make those more efficient?

Are there leaks in your bathroom? The tiniest one can waste more water than you can imagine. A leak of only 1/32" can waste over 6000 gallons of water in a month. That's 72,000 gallons in a year! Fix the leaks, no matter how small they are.

Are your pipes insulated? Insulating your pipes will save on your heating bills, as you won't have to crank the furnace up as high to ensure the pipes won't freeze. Pay attention not just to the pipes in your bathroom, but the ones under the house as well.

Install low-flow shower heads and energy saving faucets. You won't notice the decreased amount of water, and it's better not only for conservation, but for your water bill as well.

If you're remodeling your bathroom, it's the perfect time to put in a low-flush toilet.

Use a toilet dam or a plastic container to reduce the amount of water you use when you flush the toilet.

Insulate that hot water heater! If you aren't sure of what insulation to use or how to place it, hire a professional. Getting the job done right the first time will save you a lot of grief, and a lot of money over the years.

Set the thermostat on the water heater to about 130 degrees Fahrenheit (54 degrees Celsius). This is enough to kill bacteria and heat up your shower, but still save on energy.

Faucet aerators are always a good idea. You get the same amount of water pressure, but not the same amount of water flow. You won't notice the difference, but you will use much less water.

Always use a drain sieve. This prevents the problem of clogging in the future, and helps you avoid using harsh chemicals to clear the problem. To keep the drains smelling fresh without resorting to chemicals, try this: Mix one cup of baking soda and one cup of water. Pour ¼ cup into your drain, and flush it with boiling water. If you do this once a week, your drains will always smell sweet!

What if your drains do get clogged? This trick works well: Pour in ¼ cup of baking soda, followed immediately by ½ cup of vinegar. The vinegar will activate the corrosive action in the baking soda and make the whole mixture fizz and bubble. Close the drain until the fizzing has stopped, then flush it with boiling water.

As a last resort, use a pipe snake. They are available at more hardware stores and can even be rented instead of purchased. Keep in mind, however, that a pipe snake can damage your pipes!

Keep your showers short. Avoid baths! Getting a ten-minute shower uses at least two-thirds less water than a bath does.

Speaking of showers, the next time you buy a shower curtain, make it a cloth one. The usual PVC or plastic shower curtains not only clog up the landfills, they can release harmful toxins.

When you brush your teeth, don't leave the water running. You can go through a few gallons without a second thought, so make sure to turn the tap off while you brush, and turn it back on when you're ready to rinse.

Use reusable razors. In fact, go farther than that – use a razor with a metal handle rather than a plastic one. Switch out the razors when they get dull, keep them in a box, and eventually you will have enough to take down to your local recycling center.

Purchase the thin ply for your toilet paper. It is easier to disintegrate, and supports your 'less paper' usage.

Don't use disposable towels! Use cotton hand towels or handkerchiefs. Not only will they save trees, they are also easy on your face and hands. Women can also use cloth feminine napkins, as our ancestors did. They are cleaner and easier to handle than it sounds, with the washing methods used today. This alone can help our landfills from unnecessary waste.

Always use a wastebasket! Don't flush any garbage down the toilet. It can cause water treatment problems.

Make sure your soaps are entirely biodegradable and non-toxic. Homemade soap is your best bet, because you don't have any question about what went into it or the process that was used to make it.

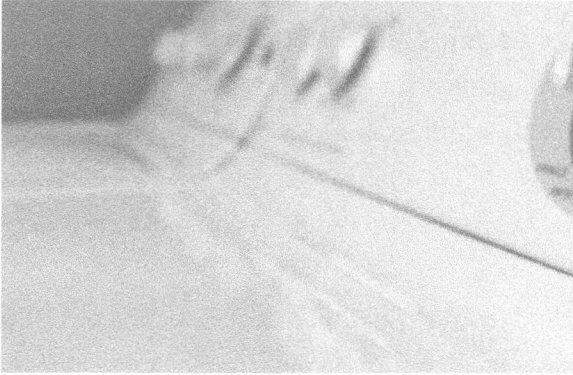

In the Laundry Room

Using harsh chemicals to clean your clothes is not necessary. The common detergents made for washing machines often contain phosphates. Those chemicals wind up in our ground water. Phosphates in our waterways act as a fertilizer, contributing to excessive growth of vegetation in the water. This chokes off the small plants and animals that depend on that water for survival.

You can use homemade soap as a detergent or try these tips:

When you are making that transition from detergent to soap, wash the items first with a bit of washing soda. This gets rid of the detergent residues, which in turn prevents yellowing of the fabrics.

When you're ready to use soap, add 1/3 cup of washing soda to the machine as it is filling up. Gradually add the clothes. Then add 1 ½ cups of soap and wash as usual.

For heavily soiled items, presoak them in warm water with ½ cup of washing soda. Leave them for at least thirty minutes. Rub the soiled areas with liquid soap before washing.

To soften fabrics, add ¼ cup of white vinegar to the rinse water.

To prevent wool from shrinking, dissolve 2 cups of salt in hot water and allow it to cool to lukewarm. Soak the garment for three hours, then rinse and drip-dry.

To wash silk, soak the garment in 1 cup of pure soap and 3 tbsp. Baking soda. Squeeze it gently after soaking and rinse it thoroughly.

To brighten clothes, don't use bleach! Try adding ½ cup of washing soda to each load to whiten the whites and brighten all your colors. Lemon juice works well, too – add it to the rinse cycle and then hang the garments in full sun. The action of the sun on the lemon juice will whiten your clothes.

But what about stains? The age-old rule still applies: The faster you treat the stain, the better your chances of removing it.

What do you do about those really tough jobs? Here are a few tips.

For soiled cloth diapers (you aren't using the plastic ones...right?), Rinse them out as well as you can. Then soak them in a solution of

3 tbsp baking soda and warm water. Do this in a tub or a washing machine, so the solution has plenty of room to penetrate all the fabric.

For fruit and wine, get on the job immediately! Pour salt or cold water on the stain and then soak it in milk before washing.

For grease stains, treatment depends on the color of the fabric. If it's a white fabric, strain boiling water through it, then follow with rubbing baking soda into the stain. For colored materials, blot with a towel, dampen with water, then rub vigorously with soap and baking soda. Wash in water that is as hot as possible, along with extra soap. (However: make sure you check the tag for washing instructions before using boiling water – it might make some clothes shrink!)

To get rid of ink, soak the item in milk, or pour hydrogen peroxide on the offending spot.

To clean your clothes of blood, immediately pour salt or cold water on the stain. Soak the item in cold water before washing it. For really stubborn stains, mix cornstarch or cornmeal with water and apply it. Allow the solution to dry, then brush it away. Wash the item thoroughly with extra soap.

For coffee and chocolate, try the magic remedy: Egg yolk! Mix the egg yolk with lukewarm water and rub into the stain. Wash as usual.

If chewing gum gets stuck to your clothes, use ice to freeze it. The gum will flake right off.

To get rid of lipstick, rub it with shortening and follow with washing soda.

If it is time to purchase a new washing machine or dryer, check out the new 'Green' machines. Using less water and products to clean your clothing, will support your efforts to have a green lifestyle. Make sure you only use non-toxic or clear cleaning products.

Run the washer only when it is full. Use the warm water cycle instead of the hot water cycle, or forget the warm water and simply use cold. Most clothes will be just as clean when washed in cold water. Be sure to check the clothing labels first, just to make sure.

Did you know that almost ninety percent of the energy used for washing goes for heating the hot water? A warm wash and a cold rinse works well for soiled clothes, and a cold wash and cold rinse works great for clothes that are lightly soiled.

For that matter, do your clothes really need washing? If it's an outer layer of clothing, such as sweaters or pants, they can be worn more than once before washing is really necessary.

Don't use your dryer if you can avoid it. Instead, hang the clothes outside on a clothesline. On a breezy day, Mother Nature will do the work, and dry them even faster than the dryer will. If it's a very cold or a wet day, hang your damp clothes on hangers, then line them up on the shower curtain rod. If you have a drying rack, use that for smaller items, such as socks. The natural flow of air through your home with dry the clothes and use no extra energy.

If you do use your dryer, there's one simple tip to keep it working efficiently: Get rid of that lint! Clean the lint trap every time you use the dryer, and every few months, clean out the hose that leads to the vent. This helps air flow and reduces the risk of fire.

Thinking about dry cleaning? Don't! Dry cleaning solvents are highly toxic. They usually include formaldehyde and chlorine, both of which are proven carcinogens. The chemicals aren't washed out of the clothes, either – they remain there after you bring them home.

Make a point of buying clothes that don't have to be dry cleaned. If you do have garments that say "dry clean only" on the tag, try washing them by hand with soap and cold water. That will usually work just fine.

If your item can't be washed by hand, take the time to find a cleaning service that offers "wet cleaning." Wet cleaning uses steam, heat, water, vacuums and natural soaps to clean your clothes. It also requires skilled workers who examine each item of clothing, so your delicate items won't be put on an assembly line of chemicals!

Non-Toxic
Cleaners

Cleaning Supplies

The aisles at the supermarket are lined with cleaning solutions that are bad for the environment. By avoiding these products and using environmentally-friendly solutions, you can do your part in saving our waterways and soil.

Each of the ingredients listed below are safe for the environment, and in some cases, might actually be good for it! They can be found in the grocery store or a health food store.

Pure Soap. Your grandparents and great-grandparents used pure soap to clean their homes and wash themselves. Pure soap is still the best way to clean your corner of the world. It is non-toxic and completely biodegradable. Since it is made of all-natural products, it doesn't harm the environment. Use a soap without any synthetics of any kind, and avoid colors and additives.

Vinegar. Used for generations, vinegar is a very versatile product. It is a mild disinfectant that combats grease, cleans glass, deodorizes almost everything, and removes stains. It is good for preventing or curing calcium deposits and wax buildup. A recycling trick is to use old newspaper to wash windows and/or glass still works.

Cornstarch. An odorless powder, cornstarch is great for cleaning carpets and rugs, and also gets out grease stains.

Washing Soda (or Sodium Carbonate). This is just what it sounds like – it is a key ingredient for washing clothes. It cuts grease, removes stains, softens water, and disinfects.

Baking Soda (Bicarbonate of Soda). Baking soda works as an abrasive. It also deodorizes, removes stains, polishes, and softens fabrics.

Here are some basic recipes for cleaning green:

All-Purpose Cleaner
½ cup pure soap
1 gallon hot water
For a sweet scent, add ¼ cup of lemon juice.

This is great for all surfaces, can be washed away with water, and is very effective for cleaning. If you want to make it stronger, double both the soap and the lemon juice.

Scouring Powder
Pure soap
Table salt or baking soda

Baking soda alone might do the trick for scouring tough surfaces, but add a bit of table salt to make cleaning easier. Add aromatic herbs, flowers or oils to your solution to make it smell nice while you clean! Put all the ingredients in a blender and swirl them to infuse the scent.
Remember to wear gloves while scrubbing. The scouring powder can be tough on your hands!

Air Freshener
It is easy to make a safe air freshener. Avoid commercial ones at all costs. You already know they harm the environment, but do you know what they do to your body? Commercial air fresheners work by masking smells, and the fine spray coats your nasal passages, deadening the nerves, thus diminishing your sense of smell.

Bet you thought the air fresheners just worked on the odors, didn't you? It actually works on your body, too – and that's not a good thing, no matter how you slice it.

Make your own air fresheners and eliminate the problem!

Use baking soda in your refrigerator and freezer. Simply open up a package and set it in the place that needs some sweetening. The baking soda will absorb the odors and leave the space smelling fresh. Replace the baking soda every few months for maximum results.

To freshen the air, dissolve 1 tsp of baking soda in 2 cups of hot water, then add 1 tsp of lemon juice. Pour the solution in a spray bottle and spritz it like you would any commercial air freshener.

The simmer pot is always a good option. Put a few slices of citrus fruit, cloves and cinnamon in a pot with enough water to cover. Simmer gently for an hour or two.

Liquid Dishwashing Soap
Even if the commercial solution is phosphate-free, it still contaminates the water. Make one of your own that doesn't have that problem. Grate a bar of pure soap into a sauce pan. Cover the shavings with water and simmer it all over low heat until it melts.

Add a bit of vinegar to the water to provide some help for the toughest grease. Cool the liquid, pour it into a container and use it as you would any dish detergent.

Furniture Polish
1 tsp lemon oil
1 cup vegetable oil

Apply it with a clean, dry rag. Use a very little bit, only what you really need, as the solution will make things slippery if it doesn't dry thoroughly.

Floor Polish

1/8 cup of paraffin wax

1 quart mineral oil

A few drops lemon oil

Melt the paraffin wax in a double boiler. Add the mineral oil and the lemon oil. Cool the mixture, then apply with a rag. Allow it to dry, then polish it with another clean, dry rag.

Glass Cleaner

4 parts water, combined with 1 part vinegar

Wash the surface with pure soap and water, then spray with the water and vinegar solution. Use an old, lint-free rag, or reusable cheese cloth or better yet-recycle an old newspaper, which cleans windows and glass exceptionally well. Don't use paper towels!

Carpet Deodorizer

To fully deodorize your carpets, sprinkle cornstarch or baking soda liberally over the surface, and allow it to sit there for an hour or so. Vacuum over the surface. Repeat if necessary.

For tough stains, try this: dissolve baking soda in a small cup of water and blot the stain with a rag. Another option is to repeatedly blot the stain with vinegar and soapy water.

Polishing Metals

Commercial polishes for metals are very harmful to the environment, and contain toxins that can be harmful to you, too. There are better ways to clean your metals.

To clean copper, try a little lemon juice mixed with table salt. Put the mixture on a rag and rub the copper. You can also use vinegar, heated up until it's warm, with a bit of salt sprinkled on.

To clean brass, try equal parts salt and flour, mixed with vinegar, rubbed on with a rag.

To clean chrome, try plain white flour on a dry rag.

Silver Cleaner

Cleaning silver is a little tougher, but it's still possible! Mix the following:

1 quart water
1 tbsp. salt
1 tbsp. baking soda
A strip of aluminum foil

Mix all the ingredients in a large pan and heat until boiling. Drop your silver in the boiling water for three minutes, then remove it and polish it with a soft cloth.

Another option is to polish your silver with a paste of wood ashes and water. Keep in mind, these methods can only be used on sterling silver. If it's silver-plated, you can ruin your items by using these tricks!

Other Household Cleaning Tips

Got a problem with rust on an item you really want to see usable again? Cover the rust spots with sour milk. To make the sour milk, combine a cup of milk with a little vinegar or lemon juice. Let the milk sit for a while, then rub the stain with salt. Place it in direct sunlight until it's dry, then wash it.

To combat mildew, pour strong soap and salt on any spots. If you can place the item in sunlight, do it – after you spray it thoroughly with vinegar. Repeat the treatment as necessary.

Remove water marks on wood furniture with vegetable oil. Using a dry cloth, rub the mark with the oil. You can also use a mixture of butter and cigarette ashes. Sounds strange, I know, but it works!

If you have a small item that has been scorched, you might be able to remove those marks. Boil the item in a cup of soap and two quarts of milk.

A Note About Safety

Many people will recommend borax and ammonia as effective household cleaners. While it's true they can do the job, it is also true that they are harsh chemicals, whether they are all-natural or not! They can irritate the nasal passage, sinuses, eyes and skin. They can also cause nausea, headaches and chest pain.

In addition, when these products are mixed with others, they can create a poisonous gas. That's why you won't find ammonia or borax recommended in this book – going green is good, but you must stay safe while doing it!

The Book On
Going Green

Have a Better Life
Through Smarter Living

Your Yard

Your Yard

If you find you must water your lawn or your garden, do it in the early morning hours or late at night. When the sun comes out, evaporation begins in earnest, so try to get as much out of every drop of water as you can by planting at times when the sun isn't out. Remember, an inch of water is better than several small showers, both for your lawn and for the environment.

What plants are native to your area? Plant those in your yard. They won't have a difficult time growing, as they are accustomed to your type of soil already.

To control weeds, use mulch or ground cover. It's a natural way of keeping your lawn or garden neat — and besides that, it's good for the soil, as it allows more air to flow to the plants who really need it.

Weed by hand as often as you can. Pesticides kill the plant but take their time in doing it, and while the plant is still alive, it can spread seeds. And of course, think of what the pesticide is doing to the ground and nearby greenery! When you pull weeds by hand, you get them out by the root, and prevent them the chance of dropping seeds nearby. That saves you a lot of work in the long run!

Put a barrel underneath your downspouts and let it fill up with rainwater. That water can be used for your garden during a dry period, or your indoor plants, or a dozen other reasons. You can also set a barrel near your garden and let the rainwater fill it up. When a few days go by without rain and you need water for the garden, it's there for the taking – and you never had to turn on a faucet.

Install motion lights on the outside of your home. Instead of using flood lights or constant-burning lights for security, install lights that only come on when they are really needed – when they detect motion around your home. Not only will you save money, the motion lights have the added element of surprise for anyone who ventures around your house at night. That surprise can be a deterrent to potential burglars or vandals.

What did we do before lawn mowers were invented? We mowed lawns the old-fashioned way: with a push mower comprised of rotating blades, kept sharp at all times. That old-fashioned mower is still available today, and with the better technology for keeping blades sharp, more efficient, light weight, it's easier than ever to maintain. Even more exciting, the amount of money saved is worth every push.

If you do have a modern mower, try an electric one. Using electric mowers help the environment by saving on the fumes and gas emitted from the machine. If you do have a mower that uses gas, keep it in optimum working condition for best efficiency.

Keep your lawn mower blades sharp. Not only does this ensure a quicker job, it helps the land. Dull blades tear the grass instead of cutting it, and once the grass plant is damaged, it will require more water to stay green.

Set your mower blades high, leaving the grass at least two and a half inches long. Anything less than that is inviting trouble in the form of weeds and disease. Longer grass also protects roots, preventing water evaporation. Consider it a blanket for your soil, and keep it a bit long.

Don't bother with that grass catcher. Leave the grass clippings on the ground. The sun and rain will break them down, forming instant compost that took no extra work. If you do use a grass catcher, empty it into your compost pile.

Creating a compost bin, not only helps your yard, but keeps it out of the landfill. Most local government centers offer the bins free. Fill up the bin with live yard clippings, food scraps and other yard materials that will decompose creating a wonderful organic soil material to put back into your garden. The reaction is truly amazing.

In drought conditions, it will be tempting to water the lawn at the first sign of browning. Don't give in to the temptation! It's only temporary, and when the rain comes again, the yard will revive.

With all this talk about your lawn, keep this in mind: A lawn is not a natural ecosystem. One plant species over a large area invites problems, such as weeds and insects. Instead of a wide, green lawn, why not plant trees for shade, flowers for beauty, ground cover instead of grass, and vegetables to feed your family? Grass isn't a necessary option, and you might even be happier without a lawn to mow!

Planting desert plants, designing a rock garden, selecting plants that do not need much water can save you in the pocketbook, while saving valuable resources. Installing synthetic grass is an alternative way to save the environment, as it is waterless and never needs to be mowed. Manufacturers now can create synthetic grass that looks and almost feels like the real thing, usually only needing maintenance once a year to take out weeds, this is a huge bonus to your 'green living.'

Pest Removal

Getting rid of unwanted pests in your home and your yard takes diligence – but it doesn't have to take harsh chemicals or solutions that hurt the environment. In fact, most of the chemical used to kill pests are very toxic to humans, too. Do you ever wonder what happens inside your body when you breathe in the fumes? That alone is enough to make the green option appealing, isn't it?

With a little time and creativity, you can avoid those chemicals altogether. Here's how:

Spiders. Let's start with the one critter you really want to keep in your house. Spiders can be your first line of defense against pests. Spiders spin their webs, catch the pests that would otherwise annoy you, and do away with them. Assuming the spider isn't poisonous, the sight of one around your house is a good thing.

Leave them alone and let them do your work for you.

Flies. The most common household pest can also be the hardest to eradicate. Sunny windows are the most common entrance to your home, so keep them closed, or keep your screens in good repair. Hang flypaper just inside your doors and windows to catch the flies that do make it inside. You can make your own with strips of yellow paper and a brush of honey.

Fruit Flies. Want to get rid of them without much effort? Get them liquored up! Pour a small amount of beer into a wide-mouthed container. Cover the container with a plastic bag and secure it with a rubber band. Poke a small hole in the bag. Flies will get in to get the beer, but then they won't be able to get out. Change the beer every few weeks and you won't have another problem with the little flies.

Cockroaches. Ah, yes. Everybody's favorite creature. The best way to keep them under control is to keep them out in the first place. Plug all small holes in baseboards, walls, shelves, and cupboards. Don't forget to plug the holes around pipes, including those around bathtub and sink fixtures. The pipes under your kitchen sink are a major entryway for roaches, so make sure those are sealed tightly.

For a trap, try greasing the inner neck of a milk bottle. Put a little beer or a raw potato in it. This will attract them, and they won't be able to get out again.

Pests in Stored Food. Pests love the convenience and delight of burrowing into your stored food, so make sure their access is limited. Store your flour, wheat, and other staples in airtight containers. For added protection, hang small cloth sacks of black pepper around the place where you store your food. For some reason, these pests – especially weevils – hate black pepper.

House Plant Pests. Pests on house plants absolutely hate the oils in peppers and garlic. You can use this to your advantage. In a small bowl, finely chop 2 or 3 very hot peppers (especially the seeds), half of a small onion, and one clove of garlic. Put it all in a pot of water, boil it, and leave it to steep for a few days. Strain it through cheesecloth and put it into a spray bottle. Spray the liquid over indoor and outdoor plants to get rid of the critters who want to eat them!

Moths. The tiny creatures get in your closets and wreck havoc on your clothes. They are attracted not to the fabric itself, but to the body oils left in the clothing after you've worn it. To make moths go elsewhere, place cedar blocks in your closets, or put cedar chips in cloth bags and hang them between your clothes. You can also use a bit of camphor dabbed onto a rag and hung in your closet. (Camphor is the active yet non-toxic part of mothballs.)

If all else fails, trap the moths. Mix one part molasses with two parts vinegar. Put it in a wide-mouthed container and set it in the bottom of your closet. Remember to clean it out regularly.

Silverfish. These pests can be caught with the same vinegar

and molasses mixture you used for the moths. They can also be repelled by treating your baseboards with a mixture of borax and sugar, or borax and honey.

Ticks and Fleas. If you have pets, you're going to have a problem with ticks and fleas at some point. Protect your pets with this simple solution: Add half a cup of dried rosemary to a quart of boiling water. Steep for twenty minutes, then allow to cool to room temperature. Spray the mixture onto your pet and let the fur dry. Do not towel him off! Once they are dry, not only are they protected from the pests that love to bite them, but they smell great.

Ants. First, find out how they are getting in! Squeeze a lemon onto that spot and leave the peel behind. Ants will go the other way to avoid it. They also avoid talcum powder, chalk, charcoal dust and cayenne pepper. Choose one and make small lines of it where you know the ants have been coming into your house. They will find someone else's house to bother!

There are companies that offer non-toxic pesticide alternatives, designed to help control the 'bugs' in your life. To find a toxin free company, go to www.thegreenlivingexpo.com for more information.

Replenish

When you take from the earth, it's imperative to give back as much as you can. Plant trees in your yard and take good care of them. Placing trees near your home, in the way of the path of the sun, will not only produce enormous and healthy trees, but it will shade your home, lowering your cooling bills.

Are you planning a wedding anytime soon? Surprise your guests with a wedding favor they can cherish for years, and one that will have a positive impact on the environment – give them baby trees. They can be purchased in bulk from the Arbor Day Foundation. They will serve as a good way to give back to the earth, as well as a lasting memory of that very special day.

Speaking of the Arbor Day Foundation, why not join up? Look into charities that provide green ideas for living and practice what they preach. You can replenish the earth all on your own, but you will have a much bigger impact if you go with someone who knows how to do it and has the means to make it all happen.

Proper Disposal

It's important to know what to do with those chemicals you used to use. You've got plastic bottles of them in the garage and the outdoor shed – but they are taking up space and it's time to get rid of them. But how do you do that without polluting the environment with the chemicals in those bottles?

Look into recycling centers in your town that offer a way to dispose of those chemicals. There are several places that will take your old bottles of motor oil, pesticides and other harmful items.

Don't try to do this yourself! Even if it appears you are pouring those chemicals into a place that is "safe," remember, no place is truly okay for these items. They will eventually pollute our lakes and streams and leach into the groundwater. Water filtration systems do a good job of removing contaminants, but despite the best efforts, a small amount of harmful chemicals can manage to get through. You don't want to contribute to the problem!

Organic Gardening

Organic gardening starts with good, clean, natural soil. Healthy soil means healthy plants. Plants that have the right nutrients to grow will always be more successful in fending off weeds, diseases, and the pests that so often plague a garden.

To make sure your soil is healthy enough, test it in early spring. It's very simple – any garden supply store will have a do-it-yourself kit. The tests will tell you exactly what your garden soil needs in order to grow the best, most healthy plants.

If your soil needs conditioning, compost is always your best bet. Compost is made up of items from your kitchen and your yard, the "brown and green" organic material that otherwise goes to waste. The organic materials in compost are broken down naturally by fungi and bacteria, and results in a nutrient-rich end product.

So don't throw it out – compost it! After a few weeks or months of adding to your organic pile, you will start to produce compost that is dark and moist. Turning the compost into your soil will improve the condition of your garden, supply beneficial organisms and nutrients.

A compost heap can be started in a corner of your backyard. If you prefer things a little neater, you can build a compost bin or purchase a compost tumbler. If you do build a bin, just remember to leave space between the wooden slats to provide good circulation, a crucial element to good composting.

To make the compost, alternate layers of garden waste and food scraps with a thin layer of soil. Keep the whole thing moist and stir it every few weeks with a shovel. Remember that the smaller the pieces are, the faster they decompose, so pull them apart if they seem to be too big.

When your compost is dark and crumbly, work it into the soil for a good general conditioner. You can add it to your gardens and lawns throughout the growing season.

The composting action will slow down during the winter, thanks to the low temperatures. If your heap freezes, that's fine – but if you want it to keep working, add a layer of plastic over the heap to insulate it and trap heat from the sun.

Don't have a big yard for composting? No problem! Even if you're in a tiny apartment in the city, you can still compost. You can start wherever you are with a simple garbage bag. In fact, compost in a bag will be more moist than outdoor piles and therefore will work faster. Simply put your small scraps of kitchen waste, a bit of coffee grounds and a few cups of top soil into a plastic garbage bag. Seal it shut and place it outside in a sunny spot. The compost should be ready to go in a few weeks.

You can also invest in an indoor composter, which sits on your kitchen counter. You simply put your kitchen scraps into it, add soil every now and then, and turn it upside down and give it a good shake from time to time. These are readily available in farm and garden stores.

When your compost is ready, you can add it to your garden outside, or use it for plants in containers.

If you're a bit more ambitious, you can look into vermicomposting. The main ingredient? Red wiggler worms! These worms are kept in a box with a bedding such as straw or grass clippings. Within a few months, the worms can create a rich, dark compost that is perfect for your budding garden.

Not sure what to put into your compost? That's the fun part – almost anything goes! Yard wastes and organic foods are good. Grass clippings, dead leaves, and shredded twigs are always good. Flower cuttings, pruned branches (shredded, of course) and weeds without the seeds are perfect. Other options include all fruits, vegetables, egg shells (crushed up first), baked goods, tea bags, coffee grounds and grains. You can even use human hair and nail clippings! Manure, hay and straw are always recommended.

What should you avoid? Don't put roots in your compost. Avoid anything that can cause harm to your plants, such as the droppings of animals, diseased plants, meats and bones, and fatty products. Don't use kitchen sauces, such as salad dressings, and avoid paper wastes. Any amount of wood ash or any toxic materials should be avoided, of course.

To make the most of your compost and help aerate your garden, use a shovel, hoe or garden rake to break up the soil. Digging in your soil is very important. It allows the roots to reach as deep as they want, without having to deal with hard-packed earth or rocks. It works well for drainage and keeps the ground aerated. It also helps get rid of harmful insects who would love to set up camp and enjoy the roots of those plants you've worked so hard to grow.

Another trick for organic gardening is companion planting. There are many plants that repel pests and help the garden stay healthy. Taking advantage of these plants is good for your garden, and prevents the temptation to buy fertilizers that are bad for the environment.

French Marigolds repel insects from your tomatoes and potatoes.

Plant collars in with your potatoes – this will discourage flea beetles.

Garlic repels many harmful insects, and can be planted with anything, except onions.

Speaking of onions, they repel many insects. You could choose to plant either onions or garlic, but not both, and still have the good results.

Plant chives near your roses. Aphids hate chives and will avoid them.

Some plants are bad for each other, such as onions and garlic. Don't plant broccoli or cauliflower close together. In fact, be careful not to plant varieties of closely-related plants in the same section of your garden, just to be safe.

Organic pesticides or barriers might work well – they are certainly worth a try!

Collars. To stop larvae from burrowing into the soil, use collars made of stiff paper or heavy tar paper. Cut a piece of about a foot square and fit it snugly around the base of the plant. Press it gently into the soil, but not deep enough that the roots don't have room to grow.

Netting. Fine netting placed over the garden bed will protect your seedlings. It will also keep cats and birds away, and prevent flying insects from laying their eggs on your garden. Cheese cloth works very well as a netting for your plants.

Insect Soap. You can find this in gardening, hardware and drug stores, and it's exactly what it sounds like – a soap that washes your plants and gets rid of the bugs.

Diatomaceous Earth. This is made from the skeletons of tiny organisms. It works by causing pests to dehydrate, leading to their death. It can be used indoors and out, but be careful – make sure to follow the directions exactly, and makes sure the diatomaceous earth you use in your home is not crystalline, or chemically produced. Those are manufactured for use in swimming pools, and that's not what you want to put on your plants! Also take care to avoid inhaling the product.

Pyrethrum Dust. This is also dangerous if inhaled, but it's very effective against soft-bodied insects, such as caterpillars. It isn't as dangerous to humans as some of the other options are.

Tobacco Water. Place a large handful of fresh tobacco into four quarts warm water. Let the mixture stand for 24 hours before use. Pour it into a spray bottle and apply it to your plants. (Warning! Even though it's all natural, this spray is poisonous to humans, so use caution when handling it.)

Hot Peppers. Blend at least three very hot peppers with ½ an onion and 1 clove of garlic. Boil this mixture in four quarts of water. Let it steep for a few days, then strain it into a spray bottle. This can also be frozen for future use.

Garlic. Mix four quarts of water with 2 tbsp of garlic juice. Don't use the garlic powder – it will burn your plants! Mix the garlic water with a little more than one ounce of diatomaceous earth and 1 tbsp. of rubbing alcohol. This can also be frozen for future use.

Soap. Putting pure soap on your plants will make them less-than-tasty to pests. To make liquid soaps, use 2 tbsp. per quart of water. To make dry soaps, use 1/5 oz per quart of water. Spray them on plants. If it hasn't rained for a few days, remember to rinse them!

When it comes to garden pests, even your best efforts might not get rid of all of them. What other option to you have? Hand-pick the offenders out of your garden! Use gloves and remove all the offending pests. Drown them in water until you are sure they have died, then dump them on the ground as a feast for your feathered friends.

Remember, those birds are your number one defense against outside pests! Make sure you have plenty of birdseed in your garden, either on cones or in feeders that attract birds. Put their favorite flowers out, too. Pincherry, honeysuckle, holly, white pine, sunflowers, and white flowering dogwood are all good choices. The birds love seeds and berries, and when they discover bugs for the taking in your garden, they will think they've found feathery heaven!

Other insects are beneficial as well. Spiders are always good for your garden, as they trap all kinds of bugs you don't want to see on your plants. Lady bird beetles, lace-wing larvae (also known as aphid lions – can you guess what they eat?), and praying mantis are all welcome additions. So are dragon flies, predacious mites, toads and garter snakes. If you see these creatures in your garden, leave them alone. By simply living in your garden, they are helping your plants thrive!

Raise bees – not only are they good for your garden, the honey makes a fantastic substitute for refined sugar in most recipes. It also helps address the problem of bees disappearing over the last few years.

The Book On
Going Green

Have a Better Life
Through Smarter Living

Transportation

Transportation

One of the most exciting areas of going green is transportation. Who would have thought just a few years ago that today we would have the number of hybrid and electric cars in general use as we do today?

The advancements in technology have been staggering and we are just at the beginning of a very exciting time, yet many people who want to turn in their old cars for the latest eco-car, just can't.

Don't despair, you can still take steps to be green even as you are forced to drive a car that many not be as efficient as you want it to be. Remember, going green is a process, not a destination so there will be a time (in the not too distant future) where everyone can have an eco-car.

Until then, try these tips:

Wash your car the natural way – wait until it rains. When the forecast calls for rain, pull that car out of the garage and let Mother Nature do the work.

If you really want to wash your car, here's a trick. Remember when we talked about lawn care, and suggested putting a barrel under a downspout to catch rainwater? You can use that rainwater for a lot of things, even using it to wash your car. Separate it out into two buckets. To the first bucket, add a bit of natural soap. Leave the second bucket with only clean water. Use the first to wash the car, and the second to rinse. You're done, and all the water it used was what you got from the clouds! Investing in waterless car wash products made with toxin free ingredients, will give you a sense of accomplishment just using a bit of elbow grease.

Avoid using your car altogether if possible. Can you walk to the grocery store? What about taking a bicycle to get your errands done? Put a big basket on the front or carry a backpack to hold the things you need to carry with you. Try the new 'green bike.' It's an electric bike, which can travel up to 20 mph for 40 miles. Rechargeable by plugging into an electrical outlet, you can bike around your entire community. Besides being good for the planet, the exercise is good for you!

If walking isn't possible, or if riding a bicycle isn't feasible, look into carpooling with a friend on a day when you both need to run errands in town. Using public transportation shows your local officials that there is a demand that needs to be filled, and may encourage them to offer broader support in this area by providing more routes, alternative options and cheaper fares.

Does your town have public transit? Many towns are moving to hybrid buses for public transportation. The bus is going in your direction anyway, so why not leave your car at home and let someone else do the driving?

Carpool to work if possible. It saves wear and tear on the car, saves the environment from the carbon dioxide your car would emit, and cuts gas prices.

Not only can you carpool to work, but you can save a ton of gas and time by forming a "school caravan." How many kids can you get safely in your car? Make arrangements to pick up kids from neighbors as you are taking your own child to school. Why use your car to drop off one kid when you can pick up others and save three or four trips for their parents? Think of the savings in gas dollars alone! Make it easier on everyone by forming a rotating schedule, and let a different parent pick up the kids each week.

If you do use your car, follow these tips to make it run more efficiently:

Keep your vehicle tuned up and in good repair. Regular maintenance helps improve gas mileage and keeps emissions down.

Change your filters regularly. Changing just the air filter can increase your mileage by up to 10%. If you are automotively challenged, just ask the dudes at the oil change shop to do it.

Topping off your gas tank can increase the amount of ground-level ozone and other air pollutants. Fill'er up, but don't go crazy, and we'll all breathe a little easier.

Keep local waterways clean by checking for leaks under the car. Just a few quarts of oil can contaminate a million gallons of water.

Make sure your tires are properly inflated. Replace your tires as recommended by the manufacturer, and have the alignment checked on a regular basis.

Change your oil as recommended. Make sure you have this done in a facility that has the proper tools and experience to dispose of the motor oil without harming the environment.

Drive sensibly on the road. Aggressive driving, such as speeding or braking quickly, will reduce fuel efficiency. It's also hard on the vehicle. Driving sensibly will save not only money, but will save you from a higher chance of having an accident.

Observe the speed limit! The optimum speed usually depends on the car, but studies have shown that gas mileage usually decreases when you top sixty miles per hour. Try using cruise control and eliminate the speed limit concern altogether.

Stop your idling, granted, not idling goes against our nature, but this is one time when it makes sense. Because modern cars don't emit nearly as much noxious fumes as the cars of yesteryear, and therefore don't stink as much, it's easy to forget about the pollution you're creating. A good rule of thumb is to turn your vehicle off if you will idle longer than 30 seconds. That includes waiting in line at your favorite drive through.

Remove excess weight in your vehicle. If you have something heavy in the trunk, get it out of there! The heavier your car, the more drag it has, and the harder the engine has to work to keep up the usual speed. This impacts smaller vehicles much more than large ones, but no vehicle gets by with added weight and no impact on the gas mileage.

Make use of overdrive gearing. When you use overdrive, your car's engine speed goes down. You will save gas and reduce engine wear, which will in turn reduce emissions.

Winterize your vehicle. The change in seasons has a great effect on your vehicle's efficiency. Take your vehicle to a service station for a tune-up and winterization, and drive confident in the fact that your car is still just as efficient in the winter months as it is in the summertime.

The Book On
Going Green

Have a Better Life
Through Smarter Living

At School or in the Office

At School or in the Office

When taking your lunch to school or work, don't use plastic bags. Keep reusable containers on hand to pack your lunch. Take your own ceramic or china cup to work with you and use that for your coffee.

Replace paper products with reusable ones.

If you buy paper, make sure it's recycled. Use paper that has not been bleached! The bleaching process to create perfectly bright, white paper is harsh on the environment, and often results in polluting the air and water. Besides that, when someone sees the darker, recycled paper, it will remind them ever-so-subtly about helping the environment.

When using paper, recycle it! Used envelopes can work well for inter-office mailings – just mark out the first address with a black marker, put your information in the envelope, and write on the white space the name of the worker or office it goes to. Drop it in the inter-office mailbox and off it goes!

When printing items for your own use, such as reports or research materials, recycle the paper by using both sides of the page. Set your printer to the smallest font you can read, and make sure there is no white space between the sections you are printing. The sheets you save will really add up!

Make sure your fax machine uses plain paper. It's almost impossible to reuse fax paper, and plain paper is better for the environment.

Do you use a courier service? Use one that employs bicyclists.

Buy one copy of the newspaper for all the staff to read. Leave it in the break room for their convenience. Better yet, encourage your employees or coworkers to read it online instead.

Take a good look at your purchasing policies. Are you purchasing your supplies from companies that have a bad track record when it comes to the environment? Shop around for companies that are more environmentally-friendly and give them your business. Explain to your old provider why you are switching, and encourage them to rethink their policies.

Weatherproof your workplace to save energy. Your boss will love the fact that the heating and cooling bills will drop, and the workplace will be a more comfortable place for everyone.

Talk to your coworkers about the environment. Set up a bulletin board where you post news about environmental concerns or important dates of meetings, rallies and government action. Set up a recycling program, too – make containers available for those plastic bottles and aluminum cans.

Use alternative materials for cleaning in the office, such as those found in this book. It is healthier for everybody in the office!

Keep your computer and all related items, such as your printer and monitor, on a single power strip. After you have shut down your computer and all related equipment, turn off the power strip. This will save energy.

When making coffee, use a permanent filter in the machine. You can buy these in cloth or mesh, and they work just as well as the disposable ones.

Install faucet aerators at work. You will cut down on water usage and the results will show in the monthly water bill.

Don't use adhesive tape! The sticky stuff can be toxic. Instead, use paperclips or staples to hold things together. Seal boxes with string. If you must use adhesive, use the stick glue or basic white glue, the kind kids use in school every day. They are non-toxic. Avoid any glues or cements that emit an odor of solvents, as those are definitely toxic to both you and the environment.

Use correction tape that covers mistakes instead of using solvents to erase them. When you do use a fluid corrector, make sure it's water-based.

Don't use markers, either. The solvent content in markers, especially those for dry-erase boards, is huge – you can tell that simply by the smell when you take off the cap. Instead, use crayons, wax pencils, or colored pencils. You can also find non-toxic markers at art supply stores. These are usually made with natural dyes.

Use pens that can be reused. Don't buy disposables! Use pens that take ink cartridges, preferably cartridges that can be refilled over and over. Purchasing a big bottle of ink and refilling cartridges uses much less material than buying one pen after another.

Instead of using bubble wrap or air cushions when you ship an item, use newspaper to protect it. Balled-up newspaper is surprisingly good at keeping things from breaking in shipment.

Pay all of your bills online, and try to keep as much correspondence online as possible. The less paper you use in sending out payments or letters, the better.

Do you really need a phone book every year? Most businesses you patronize will stay in business for years and years. Business don't normally change their phone numbers. If you need to find a number and you don't have it in your old phone book, try an internet search. When the phone company asks you if you want a new phone book this year, politely decline.

Donate magazines, newspapers and the like to your local book club or library. You can also take current magazines to your local hospital or hospice for use in their waiting rooms.

Start an environmental club at your local school. Make it a point to pick up litter around the school on a regular basis. Try to talk your class into planting a tree and taking care of it. Years later, the students can come back and look at the majestic tree they cared for when it was only a tiny seedling.

Brainstorm with the students on other ideas to make their world a more environmentally-safe place. Young people have fresh ideas and none of the pre-set boundaries that adults do, so let them go crazy with ideas! You might be surprised at what they come up with, and what will work.

Team up with your local teachers to give a short environmental lesson now and then, and relate it to what you are learning in school at the time. End the lesson with a list of things the children can do to help the environment, or help them do crafts that use recyclable materials.

Make a large sign that says, "Last one out, turn off the lights!" You would be pleasantly amazed at how many people notice the sign and take heed.
Offer incentives for your employees to carpool or use green transportation. Design your office structure to make recycling mandatory and regulate energy use. Offering incentives not only lightens the mood for 'green living,' in the workplace, but educates others on the importance of the steps you are taking.

The Book On
Going Green

Have a Better Life
Through Smarter Living

Out in the World

Out in the World

It might sound easy to reduce your environmental impact when it comes to the things you do in your own home or on your own property, but what happens when you are out in the world, in someone else's domain? You can't dictate what a grocery store, retail outlet or restaurant does – but you can decide how you will react to it.

One of the keys to success is to plan ahead. It's true that you can't control what type of wrapper a particular fast food restaurant uses, but you can control what restaurants you visit. You can also let those businesses that don't meet environmental guidelines or who aren't going green that it's important to you.

It's interesting that many businesses that just a few years ago where considered some of the unhealthiest businesses in the country are now trying to adjust their products and standards to reduce their global impact.

Clorox, a major chemical company has introduced an eco-friendly product line. McDonalds has started to include healthy choices on their menu. Many major companies throughout the world have realized that going green can make them money in the long run and have a great effect upon the planet.

What motivated most of these organizations to start being eco-responsible? Two things, customer input and profits. It doesn't matter to me what the motivation was, I'm glad they are moving in the right direction, and I believe we should identify those businesses and organizations that are attempting to do the right thing and support them. Many of my fellow environmentalists will be quick to point out that a company working to go green still has a long way to go, and they are right. Many do, but I believe it's better to reward businesses for good behavior than it is to penalize them for inappropriate behavior. Let's face it, the majority of strikes, boycotts and pickets that have a successful outcome are few and far between, but when a company sees their sales rise driven by a solid customer demand, the chances of long term success are much greater.

Shopping

Take your own bags to the grocery store. If you do have plastic bags in your house, use them over and over until they are falling apart. When those are gone, use fabric bags to carry your items. If you are going to carry items a long way, take along a backpack and fill it up. Retail companies are realizing the need to have fabric bags for their customers, which also supports them in packaging costs, when they bring their own bag to the store. Avoid excess packaging. Request paper-only packaging at the butcher counter, which takes out the need for plastic.

Plan your errands ahead of time. Map out your destinations to save transportation time and find the fastest routes.
Purchase and use stainless steel water bottles, step away from the plastic. The bottle keeps water cool or hot, while keeping unnecessary plastic out of landfills.

Choose American made or fair-trade products. Fair-trade ensures the product was made by companies that practice fair wages in fair working conditions....no 'sweat shops or child labor!'

When you purchase wine, consider buying box wines. They use less packaging and usually use less energy during shipment. However, if you have plans to reuse the glass wine bottles – perhaps for homemade salad dressing or barbecue sauce to later give away as gifts – the value of buying wine in glass bottles goes up.

Shop at thrift stores, yard sales, and clothing exchanges. Not only are the clothes and items much cheaper than what you will find at any retail store, purchasing gently used items just makes sense. Why add to the demand for new products when you can get what you need in other ways? The lower the demand for new products, the fewer of them that get made, and the less of an impact your purchase has on the environment.

When you go to the thrift store, be sure to look through your closet first. Are there clothes you haven't worn in a long while? Take those to the thrift store and donate them.

When you do look at yard sales and thrift stores, try to choose those that donate to a good cause. Many domestic violence shelters have thrift stores run by volunteers, and often the Humane Society will sponsor yard sales and the like. Not only are you doing your part to help the environment, you are helping someone in need, too.

If your community doesn't have a swap day or a free furniture exchange, organize one! How does it work? During a certain period of time, usually a weekend, the people in your neighborhood are encouraged to put things they don't want or use any longer out on the curb, with the understanding that it is free for the taking. Anyone who wants it can simply come by and pick it up. This eliminates trips to the landfill with items someone simply couldn't use anymore, and helps someone else out in the process.

Some of the biggest shopping days of the year revolve around gift-giving at Christmas time. When you have a list of people to give gifts for, it will be tempting to give in and go the easy route – simply buy something that looks good, and don't worry about how it was made or what it can be used for after the initial life of the product is over.

Why not have a gift-free Christmas? Don't exchange gifts – instead, donate a set amount to your recipient's favorite charity. Send them a card, made of recycled paper, that details what you did for them this holiday. After all, most of us don't need any more "stuff" in our lives, so giving back to someone else might be the best gift you could offer!

An added benefit of this is the lessened impact on the environment. You're not driving to the store, so you're not putting gas emissions into the air. You're not dealing with the plastic and packaging that comes with most big purchases.

Consider giving a gift of "experience." Pay for dance lessons, or give your best friend a free ticket to that cooking class. You can even give movie tickets, concert passes, and restaurant vouchers.

If you do exchange tangible gifts, consider playing "Dirty Christmas." The point of the game is to find something in your home that is attractive, worthy of giving as a gift, but something you don't need anymore. You wrap it up and take it to the party, where everyone exchanges gifts and then swaps with someone else if they see something they like better. It's great fun and doesn't cost a dime!

Some toys are toxic! Many toys are being manufactured with lead, vinyl and other toxic chemicals. Very few chemicals are banned from use, even with evidence that those materials are toxic. The government has only just begun looking at toy manufacturing. Be aware of where you shop for items, and read the labels. Not all labels give you all the information you need, so you'll have to play detective. Even self-proclaimed 'health food stores' are in the business to make money, and do not take the time to look at the toys available for sale. Don't trust someone else when it comes to your child's health.

Organize a party with your friends and ask them not to bring gifts – however, if they want to donate to a favorite charity, that's more than welcome! You will have a nice evening among people you enjoy and when it's over, you will have a nice check to present to an organization that can really use it.

How about organizing an eco-shopping trip? It's easy, and fun. Simply invite a few friends that you enjoy shopping with to ride with you to the store. You will have company on the trip and you will be saving gas by sharing the ride.

Traveling

There are millions of vehicles on the road every day, and there are just as many people flying the friendly skies. How can you lessen your impact on the environment and still have a good time on vacation?

Minimize the number of stopovers on your next airline flight. Taking off and landing cause the most emissions during the flight, so the longer you stay in the air on one plane, the better.

Try other modes of travel. A train trip through the Alps will use much less energy than using your rental car to drive the distance. As a bonus, you will meet more people who can tell you about the area. Some train trips come equipped with their own tour guide, who is more than happy to show you all the sites and answer questions. You don't get that when it's just you and your family in a car!

You can also join a carbon-offset group before you travel. These groups calculate the amount of money that would negate your carbon emissions and then help you invest it in companies that provide green energy or services for conservation. You might be taking away from the environment by your mode of travel, but you're giving back in other ways.

Millions of people stay in hotels every day. When you consider how often those sheets on the bed are changed and laundered, how many bars of fragranced soap are used only once and then discarded, and how much electricity is used in a typical hotel, the impact on the environment is staggering.

You can do your part by looking for hotels that are more environmentally friendly, and by doing some extra planning for your trip.

Try to find a "Green Hotel." These are hotels whose staff is dedicated to reducing their impact on the environment. They have implemented programs that reduce water usage, energy usage, and reduce solid waste. Hotels who participate in the green programs will give you the option of not having fresh towels, fresh sheets, or other items delivered to your room, in addition to other green-friendly options.

If you can't find a green hotel where you want to vacation, you can still do your part. Call ahead to your hotel and ask them not to put out the usual complimentary items, like shampoo and conditioner.

Bring your own eco-friendly supplies instead.

When you are at the hotel, request that they not provide room service. Is there really any need to have fresh sheets every day? You don't change the sheets on your bed at home every morning, so why should you do it when you're in the hotel?

Same with towels. You can use the towels more than once. Simply hang them on the shower curtain rod to dry after you've used them.

Look around the hotel when you get there and decide what else you can do. Is it possible to turn off the air conditioner and open the window? How about using only one of the trash cans made available, so the housekeeper doesn't waste a second plastic bag? Each hotel is different – look around and decide what you can do to make your stay a little nicer for the environment.

Restaurants

Avoid fast-food restaurants that have not made a commitment to 'green living.' Fast food can be unhealthy for you unless you make the correct choices. Some restaurants may use packaging that clogs up the landfills and wreaks havoc on the environment even though there are biodegradable choices now available today. If you do choose to purchase fast food, visit a place like Farmer's Market or Subway, where the food is wrapped in recycled or eco-friendly packaging.

Bring your own utensils. You may feel silly pulling a fork out of your purse or having the waiter use your personal coffee cup, however the rewards will far out weigh any discomfort, and you'll start feeling in control of your own life.

When you do visit a restaurant, make sure you are going somewhere that offers free-trade products. Don't be afraid to ask! If the coffee, teas or sweets they use are questionable, decline to order them. In fact, you can decline to eat at the restaurant at all – and be sure to tell the manager exactly why you are walking out the door without sampling their goods.

When you visit a restaurant, try to find one that uses their local farmer's market for produce. You can also make a point of ordering local goods from the menu. For instance, a restaurant might serve a specialty like bison meat, and they might raise the bison on the farmland next door. In a case like this, you know you are choosing something that hasn't been shipped from elsewhere, thus saving on environmental impact.

When you wash your hands at the restaurant, use the forced air dryer instead of paper towels. If there is no forced-air dryer, pat your hands dry on your pants instead of using the paper towels. Every little bit helps!
Environmentally conscious public locations, such as Dodger Stadium in Los Angeles, have hand motion dryers that start when you place your hands in them and stop immediately when you take your hands out.

The Book On
Going Green

Have a Better Life
Through Smarter Living

Activism

Activism

Going green doesn't have to stop with at your front door, at the perimeter of your yard, or even with your choices at the workplace or in the school setting. You can reach out farther than that to help the environment, and it begins with becoming active in your local community programs for recycling, environmental action and conservation.

At The Local Level

Organize a cleanup of your local beach or park. Adopt a stretch of highway and pick up litter every other weekend. Kids love to be involved in something like this. Check with your local elementary school – they might be thrilled to get the children more involved in the neighborhood. Work with your local boy scout or girl scout troop to make it happen.

Lobby for recycling stations in your neighborhood, and make sure everyone knows where they are. Ask for volunteers to help run them and make sure they are used properly. Every now and then, give the community an update, perhaps through your local paper, on the amount of recycling everyone has done.

Write letters to your local utility boards. Ask them to help spread the word about what their customers can do to save energy and conserve water. Put their tips in your local newspaper.

Start a compost or mulch exchange in your neighborhood. If you have extra mulch, give it to neighbors or to your local school to cover their playgrounds. Organic nurseries and local gardeners will pay for good compost, so you can make a small return on your investment by re-investing what you don't use. You can even start a curb-side composting program, where many members of the community get involved, and everyone has more than enough to use on their property.

What happens to all those old Christmas trees after the holiday is over? They usually wind up out on the curb or in landfills. You can fix that problem by organizing a Christmas-tree mulching program. The people in your community could bring their Christmas trees to a central location, where they are cut up into mulch. The mulch is then taken back to that person's house for their gardens, or donated to the community. It gives new life to an old tree!

Organize a tree-planting program. Trees absorb huge amounts of carbon dioxide, and they release oxygen at the same time. By doing so, they help purify the air. The more trees you have, the clearer the air will be. Start your seedlings indoors to give them a good start, and when they are big enough to hold their own, transplant them outside. Remember to put them close enough to buildings that their shade will keep those buildings cool in the summer, thus saving on cooling bills.

Start and organize an "Exchange Shed." This is a shed, carport, lean-to or the like, placed somewhere on public property in your community. It is a place where people can leave the things they no longer need, and possibly find something they can use.

For instance, do you have a set of used tires lying around, but they don't fit your new car? Take them to the exchange shed and let someone else use them instead of clogging up the landfill. This can also be used for household appliances, automotive parts, and the like. You can take old buckets of household paint there, too.

Another good place to exchange items is at your local Freecycle group. Freecycle groups have been popping up all over the country. They are usually run via email. When you have something to give away, you can offer it to the group, and give it to the first respondent. If there is something you need, ask for it! People have things in their home and shed that they never use, and they might be more than happy to brush it off and send it your way.

To find your local Freecycle group, do an internet search. If there isn't a Freecycle group near you, start one!

When you get a new cell phone, don't dispose of the old one – recycle it instead. Donate it to a women's shelter and you'll have the good feeling of knowing that somewhere, an abused woman feels safer because she has your old cell phone and the ability to call emergency services or the police if she needs to. It feels good to help the environment, but doesn't it feel delightful to help someone else out at the same time?

Ask the local schools and government buildings to put a bike rail on their property. Simply having it there will encourage more people to get out on their bikes and use them instead of cars.

Take it to city hall. Present a list of environmental questions at the next town meeting. Ask your representatives, your city staff and your caretakers about the way the city works right now. Ask them about everything you can think of that they might be able to help with. They are there to serve the community, and that includes making the community safer and greener.

Use the information they give you to suggest changes. Give copies of your findings and suggestions to everyone who might be able to make a difference – everyone from environmental groups to the governor's office. Make sure to send a news release about your findings to the newspapers and local media, too. Every little bit of exposure for going green helps!

Getting Political

Lobby politicians and local government. They are there to serve you, and sometimes, all it takes is a phone call or a letter. They love the chance to do things in the community that show good results, especially when their time for re-election rolls around. Make them aware of things they can do in your community to help the environment and beautify their area at the same time.

Buy directly from local producers. Local farmer's markets have a cornucopia of food that is fresh, ready-to-eat and grown in backyards or small farms, without any chemicals involved. You can find true organic food there, at a cheaper price than you would at the grocery store.

Best of all, you avoid the middle man. You are buying directly from the farmer, so the entire cost of your purchase goes back into the grower's pocket. They get more for their fruits and vegetables, and you get peace of mind.
Everyone wins!

Boycott companies that poison the environment. Consumer pressure and the consumer dollar speaks to companies in a way that nothing else could, and if you remove your patronage, you make them sit up and take notice.

Ask for what you want, even from the big box stores or the chain stores – they might be able to get more environmentally-safe products, but you have to ask first! Again, the response to consumer pressure will be enough to make them stock the products you want – eventually.

Push for tax cuts or rebates for those who purchase certain appliances and make green improvements, like replacing their old water heater with a high-efficiency or solar-powered one.

New political issues are popping up every day, and you can do your part. Make your voice heard! Retailers hear what you say when you wield your pocketbook, but politicians hear what you say when you VOTE.

Taking it Farther

There are many more ways to go green! Most of the ways listed in this book are simple, everyday things that anyone can do, and most of them don't have a high cost associated with them. But you can take things further – much further!

Here are some ideas for going green that involve more time, more investment, and a bit of money – but the rewards, both in long-term savings and reduced environmental impact, are enormous.

Geothermal units. These are heating and cooling units that use the power of water and the earth itself to make your home comfortable. They draw all the power your need – from your own backyard!

When the sun shines down on the earth, the ground absorbs the heat energy, up to fifty percent of it. Though the upper levels of the ground cool and warm with the seasons, the ground at a certain depth – usually about five to six feet – remains at a constant temperature year-round.

The geothermal system takes advantage of those constant temperatures. A water-based solution circulates through loops buried deep in the ground, bringing both heating and cooling to your home. Sometimes the geothermal units provide all the hot water your home needs, too – and at a substantial savings over your usual energy bill.

Geothermal units use natural methods for heating and cooling. They don't use fossil fuels of any kind! Using a geothermal system is the equivalent of removing at least two cars from the road.

Solar panels. These panels work by absorbing the light of the sun and turning it into energy. That energy is used to power homes. It's free power and it's sustainable, without any negative impacts on the environment. Solar panels used to be used only by high-tech companies and on satellites in space, but now they are becoming increasingly affordable for homes that want to reduce their environmental impact.

Green Appliances. Installing solar appliances, like a hot water heater, will have a huge effect on the environment – and on your pocketbook. Most states offer significant savings and even rebates if you choose to purchase an energy-efficient solar water heater. You can also receive a tax credit on top of the rebate. By the time you're done, between the government's "thank you" checks and your savings, that solar hot water heater has paid for itself!

Always look for the "Energy Star" seal on appliances. They are proven to be more efficient than others on the market and save you money in the long run. Look into things like dual-flush toilets, on-demand water heaters and low-flow shower heads. You can even find recycled toilet paper!

Green Cell Phones. Did you know there are cell phones in development right now that run on solar power? Motorola holds the patent, and it could very well be the wave of the future. Solar chargers for your cell phone harness the sun's energy, but also are adaptable with a hand crank option to charge your phone faster.

In the meantime, several companies are providing ways to go green even while you use your traditional cell phone. Companies like CREDO Mobile and Earth Tones are providing customers with the option of using part of their cell phone bill to invest in charities that promote environmental causes. It's a bit like buying carbon offsets when you travel, only with these companies, you're paying for those offsets when you pay your normal cell phone bill.

Electric, Biodiesel or Hybrid Cars. This is the biggest energy-saving item in the news today, thanks to rising gas prices and mumbles of an energy crisis coming sooner than anyone expected. Hybrid cars run on both gasoline and electricity; they can be hooked up to an electrical outlet and charged to perform just like a normal, gas-guzzling vehicle. They also have gas tanks, so if the electricity begins to wane as you're driving, you can still stay on the road.

Some vehicles run on biodiesel. Biodiesel is usually made from corn or soybeans. It's non-toxic and renewable, and vehicles that use it often get just as good, if not better, gas mileage than those that use traditional gasoline. While biodiesel is not widely available yet, companies are working hard to make it more accessible.

These options are just the beginning. Technology exists that would allow vehicles to run on water alone! Car companies are looking at ways to make their new cars run with better gas mileage, as well as new models that move away from using gasoline altogether. Just this year, Honda rolled out a new vehicle that puts out zero emissions. Thought it's not available everywhere yet, it's the shape of things to come.   Supposedly available within two years, keep an eye out for the new Honda FCX Clarity, which runs on hydrogen and electricity. It emits only water and none of the noxious fumes.

Every week something new is introduced as a possibility, so it's not out of the realm of logic that one year very soon, vehicles that produce zero emissions will be the norm.

The Book On
Going Green

Have a Better Life
Through Smarter Living

Cutting Through The Green Haze

Cutting Through The Green Haze

Going green can seem like a daunting task at first – there's so much to do! But with a little time and energy, you can do a good turn for the world around you. Take only what you must, replace what you do take, and always look for ways to make the world a little greener.

You don't have to sell your SUV (although it would help) and you don't have to "Go Green" all at once. As I've expressed throughout this book, going green is a process, it's not a destination.

There will always be people who feel superior or believe that they know more than you. These people believe they are better than the rest of us and can't believe that we don't hang on their every word. I believe that many of the leaders of today's environmental movement are just such people. They seem to have lost sight of the fact that businesses and individuals don't need to be bullied or threatened into doing the right thing. I believe, that once a person truly understands the benefits of going green, they are going to incorporate it into their daily lives and make it a part of their life forever.

There is a Chinese Proverb that says,

"Give a man a fish and he will eat for a day. Teach him how to fish and he will eat for a lifetime."

I believe that's what we need to do in the environmental

movement. Stop screaming and pointing fingers. Stop asking for money every time someone dreams up a new idea and simply educate people about going green.

I believe the environmental movement can make more progress by providing a solid list of benefits for people to understand rather than pushing for more government intervention. I believe we will achieve greater results through creating desire for people to conserve rather than forcing regulations on them. After all, it seems like the more the government intrudes into our daily life the more screwed up our life becomes.

The problem is, most politicians respond to the radical, vocal side of an issue rather than making the tough choice to invest money in education. After all, if our politicians aren't dreaming up regulations they feel useless.

While I don't have much faith in our political leadership, I do have faith in mankind and after all, It all begins with you!

Great Resources for Green Products

The Green Living Expo - www.TheGreenLivingExpo.com

One of the greatest ways to help build the green community is to seek out and find other like-minded individuals and businesses. The following list is a collection of organizations that I have had the privilege of working with. All have made a commitment to go green and either provide green products or provide organic and natural services.

Associations

California Department of Consumer Affairs
www.DCA.ca.gov

Cancer Control Society
www.cancercontrolsociety.com

Cancer Hope Foundation - *Evan's Charity of Choice*
www.cancerhopefoundation.org

Sahaja Yoga Meditation Center
www.sahajayogaLA.org

San Pietro Paper
www.sanpietropaper.com

Southern Nevada Water Authority (SNWA)
www.snwa.com

Food & Beverage

Adina For Life
www.adinaworld.com

Bistro Blends
www.bistroblends.com

KB West
www.21missionsgave.com

Organic To Go
www.organictogo.com

Play Food
www.playfood.org

Vons, a Safeway Company
www.safeway.com

Wholesome Cakes
www.wholesomecakes.com

Green Building

All Shades of Green
www.allshadesofgreen.net

Brighter Concepts Inc. - Solatube
www.brighterconceptsinc.com

California Green Designs Inc.
www.ca-green.com

California Solar
www.californiasolar.com

California Solar Engineering
www.calsolareng.com

CertaPro Painters
www.certapro.com/santamonica

Crown Disposal
www.crowndisposal.com

Eternaleds
www.eternaleds.com

Formula One Steam Cleaning
www.thefloorwhisperer.com

Go Green Construction
www.gogreencalifornia.com

Granite Transformations of Las Vegas
www.granitetransformations.com

GreenCart Inc.
www.coolnsave.com

Home Saving Termite Control, Inc
www.driout.com

Hybrid Light, LC
www.hybridlight.com

Ki Energy World
www.kienergyworld.com

L.A. Purification Products Inc.
www.haguewater.com

Liquid Stucco Las Vegas
www.888neverpaint.com

Liquid Stucco
www.liquidstucconv.com

Nevada Water Consultants
www.waterfreelawns.com

Nevada Water Free Lawns
www.waterfreelawns.com

No-Burn
www.noburnca.com

Pacific Home Remodeling
www.pacifichomeremodeling.com

Perform Wall
www.performwall.com

Permacity Solar
www.permacity.com

Renewal by Andersen
www.rbavegas.com

ReThink Solar- Heart and Solar Energy Unlimited
www.heartandsolar.com

Right Way Builders, Inc.
www.rwaybuilders.com

SH Architecture
www.sh-architecture.com

SoundAway Corp
www.soundaway.com

Sunburst Shutters (Reno)
www.renoshutters.com

Green Kids

Environmental Charter High School
www.greenambassadors.org

Little Green Giants
www.little-green-giants.com

Maryrose Eco Baby
www.greenbabyhome.com

Organic Keiki
www.organickeiki.com

Sprout Kids Clothing
www.sproutkidsclothing.com

Veronica Lane Books
www.veronicalanebooks.com

Green Living

100 Fires Books
www.100fires.com

A-1 Organics Nevada LLC
www.a1organics.com

Absolute Paradise Landscaping

www.paradiselawnlv.com

Ameriprise Financial Services, Inc.
www.ameriprize.com

Bamboo 2000
www.bamboo2000.com

Bamboo Moon Inc
www.bamboomoon.net

Bio-Planet Products L.L.C.
www.bioplanetproduct.com

BuyGreen.com
www.buygreen.com

Chi Herbal Formulas
www.chiformulas.com

Conservation Services Group
www.premiumcooling.com

Culligan Water Conditioning
www.culligan.com

DNC, Parks & Resorts at Yosemite
www.tenayalodge.com

Dr. Banker
www.drbanker.com

Dragon Herbs
www.dragonherbs.com

EarthRehab

www.earthrehab.com

Eco Smart Home Water
www.ecosmarthomewater.com

Eco Totables
www.ecototables.com

Eco Zen Boutique
www.ecozenboutique.com

Eco-Absorb
www.eco-absorb.com

Empire Solar Solutions
www.empire-solar.com

Environmental Motors. Com
www.environmentalmotors.com

Ethos For Earth
www.newgreenalternatives.com

Eurolaces
www.eurolaces.com

Exotika Fashion
www.exotika.etsy.com

G.E.I.- Ongoji.com
www.ongoji.com

Got LV Real Estate.com
www.gotlvrealestate.com

Green Clean

www.greencleanla.com

GreenerPrinter
www.greenerprinter.com

Hemp Queen
www.hempqueen.com

Hollywood Paws
www.hollywoodpaws.com

Hometown Products
www.toiletta.com

Hybrid Roots- Roots Dog
www.hybridroots.com

Hydro Dynamics
www.ehydrodynamics.com

JPS Global Investments
www.jpsglobalinvest.com

June Accessories
www.juneaccessories.com

Kinetico
www.kwater.com

LA Water Works
www.lawaterworks.net

LED Insider
www.ledinsider.com

Life and Wellness Network

www.lifeandwellnessnetwork.com

Life Source Water Systems
www.lifesourcewater.com

Live Green Realty
www.livegreenrealty.com

Livity Outernational
www.livity.org

Maid Brigade
www.swlasvegas.maidbrigade.com

Modern Earth
www.modern-earth.com

Mother Earth
www.motherearthcleaning.com

MPS Rainbow
www.mpsrainbow.com

MWD / Save Water, Save A Buck
www.bewaterwise.com

My Forever Green
www.myforevergreen.org/7876

Natural Energetics
www.naturalenergetics.com

Origin Laboratories
www.purosol.com

Patterson Sales Agency

www.pattersonsales.com

Prevailing Windpower
www.prevailingwindpower.com

Price-Pottenger Nutrition
www.ppnf.org

Quantum Biofeedback / Project by Project
www.projectbyprojecthealth.com

Rain Frog Apparel
www.rainfrogapparel.com

RCC Solar
www.rccsolar.com

RMD, Inc.
www.suportbyrmd.com

Royal Prestige - Hicite
www.cook-works.com

Shaklee Distributor
www.shaklee.net/brad_hudson

Sleep & Beyond
www.sleepandbeyond.com

So Easy 3-Day Colon Cleanse/ Ins-USA/Easy Pha-max
www.christian16.easyphamax.biz

Soul Notes
www.iamsoulnotes.com

Sun and Shade

www.sbebc.com

Tasmanian Rain
www.aduroadamo.com

The Eleanor Group
www.theeleanorgroup.com

The Fifth Element Himalayan Salt of the Earth
www.thefifthelement.biz

The Green Game
www.admcadiam.com

The Inconvenient Bag + Sahara Clinic
www.theinconvenientbag.com

Toyota/Scion of Hollywood
www.lacarguy.com

Waterless Turf (Synthetic Grass)
www.waterlessturf.com

Welk Resort Group
www.welkgroup.com

Welltrients for Life
www.welltrientsforlife.com

WorldMark by Wyndham
www.wyndhamworldwide.com

Wowzzy.com
www.wowzzy.com

YourTurf, Inc.

www.yourturf.com

Health & Beauty

Arbonne
www.arbonne.com

Arbonne International
www.indulge.myarbonne.com

Bioken Natural Antibiotic
www.thebioken.com

Color Therapy Eyewear
www.colortherapy.com

Creative Airs
www.creativeairs.com

EcoUsable, Inc.
www.ecousable.com

Energy Essentials
www.energyessentials.com

Amazon Drops
www.amazondrops.com

Golden Earth
www.goldenearth.net

Graceful Earth, Inc
www.gracefulearth.com

Healer's Guide, LLC
www.healerguide.com

Healing Heat
www.healingheat.com

Illumination Arts Publishing
www.illumin.com

Knowledge 2 Home Wealth
www.myverve.com/knowledge2homewealth

Making You Custom Blend Cosmetics
www.youcosmetic.com

Mona Vie
www.monavie.com

My Herbal Muse
www.myherbalmuse.com

Nikster LLC
www.niksters.com

Omica Health
www.omicahealth.com

Pure Life
www.purelife.citymax.xom

Pure Necessities
www.purenecessities.net

SeneGence International
www.senegence.com/smearnomore

Sensaria
www.sensaria.com

Suds in a Bucket
www.sudsinabucket.com

The Designer Com
www.cenresusa.com

The Massage Express Co.
www.themassageexpress.com

This™... Naturally
www.thisnaturally.com

Up Dog Down Dog Yoga
www.updogdowndogyoga.com

V'tae Parfum & Body Care
www.vtae.com

Xango
www.mymangosteen.com/carp

Yoga Groove
www.yogagroovestudio.com

Z-ION Cleanse
www.z-ioncleanse.com

Organic & Natural Products

Be Well Products
www.organic-gourmet.com

Bonne Santee / Salad Master
www.saladmaster.com

FaeriesDance.com
www.FaeriesDance.com

Holistic Health Center Inc.
www.organicasbotanica.com

Lotus Blossom Style
www.lotusblossomstyle.com

Melaleuca
www.melaleuca.com

Physician Formulas, Inc.
www.organicwearmakeup.com

Pure Fiber
www.pure-fiber.com

Spenger System Inc. - Bistro Blends
www.spenger.com

ChicoBag Company
www.chicobag.com

The Green Girls

Eco-Sapian:
A human that wants a better life by caring for the planet.

Green Girls:
Women joined together to educate and promote the green revolution.

As passionate green advocates, The Green Girls share their tips, ideas and latest news to not only go green, but save green. The Green Girls consists of Jami, Jess, Patty, Danni, Becky and Shari who preach that going green is doing anything that you can and even one step is a step in the right direction.

Whether its the result of human neglect or natural cyclical patterns, it is everyone's obligation to make an effort to slow the negative effects of the global climate crisis we are currently experiencing. There is no question that Global change is happening and while it may not be entirely detrimental, we are focused on encouraging everyone to do their part to reduce their carbon footprint and be conscious of their daily actions.

Don't miss The Green Girls segment every Saturday on The Green Living Hour with Evan Albright from noon to 1pm on KHVN 830 AM Hawaii. Or Money Intelligence with Ken and Katie KKZZ AM Ventura every Thursday from 2:00pm to 4:00pm for their designated Green Day, where the Green Girls will share their latest in eco-tips and ideas.

Eat Green, Drink Green, Wear Green, but most of all Live Green!